Praise for *The Glance*

"Barks's translations are justly famous for their bell-like clarity and sharp simplicity. A highly desirable book, in all senses of *desire*."
                                        —*Booklist*

"Barks's ear for the truly divine madness in Rumi's poetry is truly remarkable."
                                        —Huston Smith

THE GLANCE

Coleman Barks was born and raised in Chattanooga, Tennessee, and was educated at the University of North Carolina and the University of California at Berkeley. He taught poetry and creative writing at the University of Georgia for thirty years. Coleman Barks is the author of numerous Rumi translations and has been a student of Sufism since 1977. His work with Rumi was the subject of an hour-long segment in Bill Moyers's *Language of Life* series on PBS (1995), he is a featured poet and translator in Bill Moyers's poetry special, "Fooling with Words" (1999). Coleman Barks is the father of two grown children and the grandfather of three. He lives in Athens, Georgia.

Rumi

THE
GLANCE

Songs of Soul-Meeting

TRANSLATED BY

Coleman Barks

WITH

NEVIT ERGIN

PENGUIN COMPASS

PENGUIN COMPASS
Published by the Penguin Group
Penguin Putnam Inc., 375 Hudson Street,
New York, New York 10014, U.S.A.
Penguin Books Ltd, 27 Wrights Lane, London W8 5TZ, England
Penguin Books Australia Ltd, Ringwood, Victoria, Australia
Penguin Books Canada Ltd, 10 Alcorn Avenue,
Toronto, Ontario, Canada M4V 3B2
Penguin Books (N.Z.) Ltd, 182–190 Wairau Road,
Auckland 10, New Zealand

Penguin Books Ltd, Registered Offices:
Harmondsworth, Middlesex, England

First published in the United States of America by
Viking Penguin, a member of Penguin Putnam Inc. 1999
Published in Penguin Compass 2001

3   5   7   9   10   8   6   4

THE LIBRARY OF CONGRESS HAS CATALOGED
THE HARDCOVER EDITION AS FOLLOWS:
Jalāl al-Dīn Rūmī, Maulana, 1207–1273.
[Divan-i Shams-i Tabrīzī. English. Selections]
The glance : Rumi's songs of soul-meeting / translated
by Coleman Barks.
p.   cm.
Includes bibiographical references.
ISBN 0-670-88755-2 (hc.)
ISBN 0 14 10.0231 X (pbk.)
I. Barks, Coleman.   II. Title.
PK6481.D6E5   1999
891.55'—dc21   99–25074

Printed in the United States of America
Set in Guardi
Designed by Francesca Belanger

For the mystery of the Friend

Contents

Introduction

A Soul-Friendship

The Meeting

WHEN I FIRST VISITED KONYA, Turkey, in 1984, I went by my-
self. I wandered the streets, wrote, and worked on the ver-
sions of Rumi I was beginning to publish. It was a peaceful
time for me. Konya is a town with two centers: Rumi's tomb
and the dervish museum there, and the much more spare
building where Shams is probably *not* buried. I got to be
friends with the keeper of Shams's tomb. Wherever I would
sit on the floor against the wall to do my writing, he would
come and politely realign me. I was never quite situated to
suit him, and I was grateful for the attention. I rarely spoke to
another human being inside the ellipse of those two weeks.

It was Ramadan. I did what the town was doing. I fasted
from sunup until sundown. At about eight in the evening
I'd step into a restaurant and sit with everyone waiting for
the call from the minaret, when each person dips a spoon
into the lentil soup. Each night I ordered bottled water
with my meal, but my Tennessee Turkish seemed to draw
a crowd. People came out from the kitchen and solemnly
listened to me order. It was not until I got home that I found
out that what I'd been ordering with every meal was *the secret
of the universe. Sir* instead of *su.*

The central point in the lives of both Jelaluddin Rumi and
Shams of Tabriz was their meeting in 1244. Deep friend-

ship, poetry, and a community of dervishes generated from that core. Rumi approached the moment from a lineage of scholars, jurists, theologians, and mystics. He was born near Balkh, Afghanistan, in 1207, on the eastern edge of the Persian empire. As a young man he left that region permanently with his family, fleeing just ahead of the invading Mongol armies of Genghis Khan. They settled in Konya, his father the head of a dervish college, a position Rumi took over on his father's death. In addition to this traditional education Rumi also received extensive mystical retreat training from the Sufi master Burhan Mahaqqiq.

Shams was from Tabriz in western Persia and he also had a teacher, Ruknuddin Sanjabi, but his path was less definable. He wandered the Near East in search of a spiritual companion. In between times of absorption in mystical trance, he would work as a mason or at some other physical job. When students gathered around him, as they inevitably did, Shams would wrap himself in his black robe and leave. He was known as Parinda, "the winged one." In a moment of deep longing he asked if there was a companion for him. A voice came: "What will you give?"

"My head."

"Jelaluddin of Konya is your friend."

Rumi's poetry came out of the great friendship of Rumi and Shams. There are several versions of their initial meeting in 1244. One is simply that they glanced at each other. Another, that they talked about Muhammad and Bayezid Bistami. The one I love involves a drowning of books. Rumi is sitting by a fountain in a small square in Konya reading to students from his father's dazzling spiritual diary, the *Maarif*. Shams breaks through the group and throws the invaluable text, along with other books on the pool's edge, into the water. "Who are you and what are you doing?" asks Rumi.

"It is time for you to live what you've been reading," replies Shams. Rumi turns to the books in the water. "We can retrieve them, if that's what you want," Shams says. "They will be perfectly dry, just as they were."

Shams lifts one out to show him. Dry.

"Let them stay," Rumi responded.

We probably cannot imagine what that relinquishing meant in the thirteenth century. A book must have felt like such a rare, complex entity, as subtle and labyrinthine as a town. To give them up would have been a deep surrendering.

So began the friendship that became a way. Perhaps there is a necessary break between text and sacred experience. To go deeper, Rumi had to abandon his books. Rumi keeps saying this in almost every poem: words are not it. Language is not living. Rumi and Shams went off into months-long periods of *sohbet*, the twin-nova conversational dance that had such tremendous creative energy. A kind of force field of a crackling vitality. We don't perhaps have a parallel in the West: Don Quixote and Sancho Panza, Jesus and Mary Magdalene, Faust and Mephistopheles, Lear and Cordelia, Suttree and Harrogate, each pairing has its own quality, but with Rumi and Shams the spiritual stakes are raised considerably. It's Rumi's pilgrim heart with Shams's fierce intelligence, the one from the soul line of Jesus, the other the unpredictable spiritual assassin. The gentle gatherer up of animals and children, the hero of dogs, matched with the elusive wild wanderer. They came together so well that they created a new mysticism.

The double story of the lives of Rumi and Shams is that they found in each other the indescribable *third script*, which cannot be understood with mind but is known only as another person is known, as a presence is felt. Shams once said,

> The writing comes in three scripts.
> One that he and only he can read.
> One that he and others can read.
> And one that neither he nor anyone else
> can read. I am that third script.

The friendship that Rumi and Shams embodied was clear and miraculous and essential, like water.

But some in the Konya community felt jealous of the friendship. They plotted to force Shams away and eventually they killed him and hid the body. Rumi wandered looking for Shams until one day in Damascus he realized that Shams was within him. There was no need to search anymore. Rumi himself embodied the friendship. With that illumination he returned and began speaking the spontaneous poetry that is loved across the world. All of it can be overheard as a conversation with Shams of Tabriz.

The Glance

THE NIGHT BEFORE Leonard Bernstein died he asked that several poems from the *Like This* volume of Rumi's *Divan* be read to him over and over. His friend Aaron Stern wrote to me about that night. The poems seemed very fresh and familiar to Bernstein.

This poetry is from the thirteenth century, of course, and yet it does seem to be a *new* kind of love poetry. It's been seven centuries, but maybe we are just now beginning to assimilate the essence of the friendship that Rumi and Shams brought to the mystical life of the planet. Body and soul terminology here dissolve. Even the word *love* may be wrong for what Rumi and Shams share. Their friendship widens to include the sun, the fields, and "anything anyone says" (p. 44). It is a kind of atmosphere that they inhabit. The place they reach is where, in some way, they are not, where absence, or a vastness, is. Perhaps *love* isn't the word for it. Something greater than the personal opens, burns, and rises through. It cannot be understood or described, but it can be *lived*.

There is a mystery called the glance, the gift, *nazar*. For nine years I visited a great teacher's room in Philadelphia. Whenever I sat in Bawa Muhaiyaddeen's presence, I felt the deep truth of the place we were living within. When I consciously felt *All this is happening inside*, he looked over at me and smiled as though to say *Yes*. I first encountered him on May 2, 1977, in a dream, before we met in the Philadelphia room. The dream notebook I kept then describes it as a waking up inside my dream. A ball of light above me was clarifying from the center outward. A man sat cross-legged inside the sphere of light. He (Bawa) raised his head and said to me, "I love you." I said the same to him and the landscape, the curve of the Tennessee where I grew up, where I was in the dream, felt saturated with love as with dew. That's all that happened in the dream. Bawa's favorite term of endearment for those who came to his room was "the precious jeweled lights of my eyes." The sanctuary of the glance. A haven, like a ship or a garden. Another Indian teacher, Meher Baba, used to indicate that those near him were living in the protection of his *nazar*. I don't think it matters whether one has a living teacher or not, one can still live in the glance of the soul guide, the inner friendship. A wonderful statement of that enveloping vision is Rumi's line,

I see my beauty in you.

A spiritual alchemy takes place inside the glance. Desire changes and becomes a continuous moment.

Rumi's big volume, the *Divan-i Shams-i Tabriz* (*The Works of Shams of Tabriz*, sometimes called just *The Shams*) expands the concept of the love lyric into a region where many languages blend: the jewel imagery of mysticism, clouds of bewilderment, the charge of erotic language, and the feel of drunkenness. The wine-surge around a table of friends was something Rumi knew well. It's a new and old mixture of human desirings, longings, and other intensities. These poems come from a place where those experiences are both felt and transformed. The realm of the glance is beyond touch, and somehow within touch too. The friendship of Rumi and Shams goes past wantings, past ideas of gender, beyond the old love categories, beyond the synapse of the garden balcony scene, and beyond mind. It can only be experienced in the place where all connect, where the enlightened ones live, and in what they become part of when they die. Dewdrop *does* become ocean. Universal consciousness builds. Soul work is everyone's purpose and freedom. As the Qur'an says, "All shall be brought into the presence."

I want to be careful not to be dishonest or hypocritical about my own life in relation to this poetry. By some external standards I've led a scandalous life: lots of lovers, lots of wine drinking, lots of unconsciousness. God knows, I have loved sex and still am drawn to it. But the focus of my loving has moved upward some, since I was in my thirties, forties, and fifties, to the chest, the throat, the forehead. That's age, maybe, rather than kundalini, energy, work. But from the inside, in my day-to-day activities I mostly feel a tender earthiness, a camaraderie with the attention I see people giving their trying. Other times I'm distracted, cautious, unpeaceful, uninterested, or caught up in my self-lacerating, soap-opera personality. That's fairly rare at this point in my life. I love music and meditation, but I'm not faithful with practices—except the poetry. I turn to that on a regular basis. I do not live in a mystically radiant state, though I've had experiences that I treasure and cannot explain. More than several times a day I remember with the Sufis, *There is no reality but God.*

The only authority I claim for being able to work on Rumi's words is that I was told to do so by one who was on the same level of awareness as Rumi's and the leader of a similar learning community, the one in Philadelphia with Bawa in the 1970s and '80s. When I work on bringing these poems over into American English, I feel restored to the presence of teachers; I touch a bedrock state beyond my moodiness and my mind. I connect with my experience, however partial, of the friendship, the *sohbet*, that is the subject, the air these poems breathe. I have had my defining moments with Bawa, in dream and out, moments in meditation, and other times with friends. I agree with Osho Rajneesh that a truth not lived is not a truth. But maybe this friendship and the poetry of it can be grown into gradually.

I wait beside these poems with a kind of heart-listening. And it feels right to acknowledge that although I am working on the words of an enlightened being, I am not one. If I were in the station of Rumi and Shams, I'd probably be spontaneously making my own anonymous poetry. I'm not the cook, more a strangely elated waiter bringing out dishes. I hope I am able at times to be the empty screen on which Rumi's joy and grief can play. These poems are beyond me. That's why I love working on them. They draw me where I have to go.

Nevit Ergin, the Turkish teacher whose literal translations into English form the basis of this work, was told by his teacher, Hasan Sushud, that of all texts, Rumi's *Divan* was the best guidebook to mystical annihilation, which is certainly the core teaching of all the world's religions: the dissolving of personal conditioning that is the key to becoming a true human being. The merging of the two oceans of Rumi and Shams recorded in the *Divan* is the music of that annihilation.

Amazingly, of Rumi's *Divan* only about a third has been brought over into English from the Persian (see the note on Nevit Ergin's work at the end of this volume). From what we have so far (perhaps a thousand out of three thousand), the *Divan* does seem to launch love poetry into another dimension. In literary terms, of course, these poems do grow from the same soil that produced the Provençal love lyric and the troubadour tradition, as well as from the ecstatic mystical traditions. There's a lot of overlap. Without getting too literary, you could say that both traditions use many of the same images (nightingales, roses, wine, gardens, swords, knots, dawn, rubies, springwater, doorways) and examine some of the same subjects (the source of song, the qualities and powers of love, the unsayable name of the beloved, a general questioning of language, a celebration of the spirit's incarnation, and the intensity of the present moment). Rumi's *Divan*, though, takes this mixture of love and ecstatic devotion onto a plain of absolute emptiness. It has none of the irony and self-conscious artifice of courtly love, where the jokester and his bitterness are never forgotten. In Rumi there's laughter but it's not the undercutting kind; it expresses a grand inclusive health. The anticipated event in the *Divan* is a meeting with the Friend: the discovery of one's wild true nature. The longed-for encounter is with the one dressed in "the flower of God's qualities, / not your torn robe of self-accusation" (p. 21).

One of the first things that Bawa asked me in his room in the Overbrook Avenue house was, "Will you meet me on the inside or on the outside?" I answered from my English-teacher mind, "Isn't it always both?" He picked at the covers where he sat on his bed and held me in his eyes.

> Face that lights my face, you spin
> intelligence into these particles
>
> I am. Your wind shivers my tree.
> My mouth tastes sweet with your name
>
> in it. You make my dance daring enough
> to *finish*. No more timidity! Let
>
> fruit fall and wind turn my roots up
> in the air, done with patient waiting.
>
> (p. 51)

Twenty years after Bawa's question that Rumi poem would be a truer answer. The dance-glance happens each moment and the moment keeps renewing itself, changing along with the conversation. Rumi often seems to contradict or oppose himself in these poems. Perhaps how the soul grows toward God cannot be spoken of rationally. For example, sometimes Rumi celebrates the soul's containment in desire and imagination, other times, its release into meditation and peace. The saddlemaker's work ("Be a slave to / the ground!" p. 67) is praised as well as the falcon's liftoff into emptiness and freedom. Blood is better than wine sometimes. The soul's joy is found in a human eye. Rumi does not resolve contradictions so much as he sings them. He lives in them. Incarnation is not a dungeon, but a closed box of musk getting muskier. The smallness of the play area is a strength! Particles turning in tiny orbits compose the diamond we inhabit. Rumi is in these poems, enduring and enjoying the many contradictions: the sweetness of grief, the freedom of limits, the warmth of going naked, the eloquent silence.

The feel of union and separation at once. Rumi and Shams *met* on a street in Konya in late October 1244, and somehow their way of friendship continues to open and reveal itself for each generation of loved ones, be it man and woman, child and grandparent—any bond. The last question I asked Bawa before his death on December 8, 1986, was about his eyes. "Will what I see in your eyes ever come up behind mine and look out through me?" He used that most profound pun in English to answer. "When the *I* (eye) becomes a *we*." My strongest memory of the rainy afternoon we buried Bawa is of the amazing light in everyone's eyes. Enlightened beings who live their souls so deeply surely continue to live in the eyes of those who love them. It is my feeling that we are given in Rumi's poems glimpses of the world of *sohbet* that Rumi and Shams opened. We hear them living the mystery of being free *and* tethered. Free enough to complain directly to the source of inspiration. "What have you been / drinking that you want so many ecstatic / poems?" (p. 78), yet still tied in the barn of words.

As the last poem in this selection shows, these were part of a learning community's practice. They were used in *sama*, the listening sessions where music and poetry and movement wove together human and divine. In the community I was part of, Bawa would sometimes look around the room for long minutes, from person to person. The quality of compassion, the silent gift of the glance, almost audible. Surely one of the great messages of Rumi's poetry is how we carry in us the joy and the depth of the friendships we've lived, and how we give that away.

The Ghazal

A GHAZAL can be from eight to forty lines long, or longer. Traditionally, it has been composed of autonomous couplets (rhyming *aa ba ca*, etc.) that leap inexplicably from thought to thought, image to image. The subject is love, mystical longing as well as human love. The *ghazal* is passionately unstable, and beautifully suited to mirror a mixture of longings. I have used the coupleting of lines here to give a feel of contained spaciousness to the free verse, except in the spring conversation poems (pp. 47–50) and the poems about musical modes (pp. 53 and 55). In those the lineation is more whimsical. In the musical-mode poems the poetry is evidently being spoken along with changes in musical styles. Rumi was close to his musicians and may have played an instrument himself. He uses the interlocking of musical modes as another sort of conversation, and a form of *zikr*, the remembering that *there is no reality but God. There is only God.*

The classical *ghazal*, which took form in Persian (and later in Urdu, Turkish, and Arabic) in the eleventh and twelfth centuries, was melancholy in tone, lamenting separation from the loved one. Rumi's tone is different. His comes out of a lovingness that acknowledges the presence as well as the absence of the beloved, and a conversation (*sohbet*) that is the essence of both beings. At the end of each poem, where the traditional *ghazal* mentions the poet's name as a kind of signature, Rumi invokes Shams, or Saladin Zarkub, or silence, or sunlight itself.

I recently went to a van Gogh exhibit. His vision made me feel the truth of the Rumi poetry. The exhibit concentrated on the last three years of van Gogh's life, when he did almost a painting a day. He saw the fields and gardens and houses, the pot of basil, the old shoes, beached boats, and his own bedroom as drenched in amazing colors and shot through with light. I'd say with God. Van Gogh's world is not hyper. It's how it *is*. The same with Rumi's *ghazal*s. He feels the glory of a morning wind, a drink of water. Smiling, speaking, laughter, music! The ecstatic world is not an abnormal state. It's where these three hundred billion galaxies turn, and the dogs bark, and trees move their limbs so delicately, and the birds sing! Rumi hears what they're singing continuously as *Show yourself to us!*

Rumi spoke these poems as spontaneously as birdsong. They came impromptu as part of his work with his community. The work was the work of opening the heart and exploring the mysteries of friendship and absence, of surrender and discipline. His scribe, Husam Chelebi, wrote them down as they came, and so recorded a human voice in the moment of its dissolving in the divine *You*. These poems were to be heard with music. Music was part of the practice of the dervishes. In Persian the poems can be sung as well as read. And music is often a metaphor for what connects human beings in the ocean of consciousness. Music is, as Rumi says (p. 53), a form of *zikr*, the remembering that *There is no reality but God. There is only God.* In Arabic, *La 'illaha il' Allahu.*

THE
GLANCE

Jars of Springwater

Jars of springwater are not enough
anymore. Take us down to the river!

The face of peace, the sun itself.
No more the slippery cloudlike moon.

Give us one clear morning after another
and the one whose work remains unfinished,

who *is* our work as we diminish, idle,
though occupied, empty, and open.

The Taste of Morning

Time's knife slides from the sheath,
as a fish from where it swims.

Being closer and closer is the desire
of the body. Don't wish for union!

There's a closeness beyond that. Why
would God want a second God? Fall in

love in such a way that it frees you
from any connecting. Love is the soul's

light, the taste of morning, no *me*, no
we, no claim of *being*. These words

are the smoke the fire gives off as it
absolves its defects, as eyes in silence,

tears, face. Love cannot be said.

An Invisible Bee

Look how desire has changed in you,
how light and colorless it is,

with the world growing new marvels
because of your changing. Your soul

has become an invisible bee. We
don't see it working, but there's

the full honeycomb! Your body's height,
six feet or so, but your soul rises

through nine levels of sky. A barrel
corked with earth and a raw wooden

spile keeps the oldest vineyard's wine
inside. When I see you, it is not so

much your physical form, but the company
of two riders, your pure-fire devotion

and your love for the one who teaches you;
then the sun and moon on foot behind those.

A General Introductory Lecture

A nightingale flies nearer the roses.
A girl blushes. Pomegranates ripen.

Hallaj will be executed. A man walks
a mountain path, solitary and full of

prayer. Trust grows for nine months,
then a new being appears. Narcissus

at the edge, creekwater washing tree
roots: God is giving a general intro-

ductory lecture. We hear and read it
everywhere, in the field, through the

branches. We'll never finish studying.
Neither of us has a penny, yet we're

walking the jewelers' bazaar seriously
considering making a purchase! Or

shall I say this with other metaphors?
A barn crowded with souls. Quietness

served around a table. Two people talk
along a road that's paved with words.

Hamza's Nothing

A moth flying into the flames says
with its wingfire, *Try this*. The wick

with its knotted neck broken tells you
the same. A candle as it diminishes

explains, *Gathering more and more is
not the way. Burn, become light*

and heat and help, melt. The ocean
sits in the sand letting its lap

fill with pearls and shells, then empty.
The bitter salt taste hums, *This*.

The phoenix gives up on good-and-bad,
flies to nest on Mount Qaf, no more

burning and rising from ash. It sends
out one message. The rose purifies

its face, drops the soft petals, shows
its thorn, and points. Wine abandons

thousands of famous names, the vintage
years and delightful bouquets, to run

wild and anonymous through your brain.
Empty, the flute closes its eyes

to Hamza's nothing. Everything begs
with the silent rocks for you to be

flung out like light over this plain,
the presence of Shams-i Tabriz.

The Verge of Tears

You make our souls tasty like rose
marmalade. You cause us to fall flat

on the ground like the shadow of
a cypress still growing at its tip.

Rainwater through a mountain forest,
we run after you in different ways.

We live like the verge of tears inside
your eyes. Don't cry! You trick some

people with gold ropes, tie them up and
leave them. Others you pull near at dawn.

You're the one within every attraction.
All silence. You are not alone, never

that, but you must be distracted, because
look, you've taken the food you were

going to give Jesus out to the stable
and put it down in front of the donkey!

Grainy Taste

Without a net, I catch a falcon
and release it to the sky, hunting

God. This wine I drink today was
never held in a clay jar. I love

this world, even as I hear the great
wind of leaving it rising, for there

is a grainy taste I prefer to every
idea of heaven: human friendship.

Tambourine Feet

When you are not with me, I sometimes
resemble a fish put live in the skillet,

writhing its little cooking time left,
or the empty eyes of graffiti faces, or

a house with no one home. Other times,
my love for your soul spreads out over

the city like music. Quadrant to quadrant
the jeweled tambourine feet move, palace

to ghetto. The cultured, the craftsman,
the slave, all begin to hum and sing *this*.

The Mirror Between Us

The mirror between us is breath
mist when I speak. Your face

in water: I reach, the work
grows muddy. Even *friend* and

beloved are wrong words for this.
Even *ahhhhh* retreats back into

my mouth, the same if the moon's
behind cloud or being released.

A pure silent look is better.

In Love that Long

I am here, this moment, inside the beauty,
the gift God has given,
our love:
> this gold and circular sign
means we are free of any duty:
> > out of eternity
I turn my face to you, and into
eternity:
> we have been in
love that long.

Green from Inside

The moon comes to visit as a guest
of the night. Rose sits down by

thorn. Someone washing clothes
asks for the sun's forgiveness!

Compass leg circles the point.
Muhammad arrives here, a stranger,

Spring to this dry tree. Hallaj
smiles at his cross. The pomegranate

flowers. Everyone talks about
greenery, not with words but quietly

as green itself talks from inside,
as we begin to live our love.

I See My Beauty in You

I see my beauty in you. I become
a mirror that cannot close its eyes

to your longing. My eyes wet with
yours in the early light. My mind

every moment giving birth, always
conceiving, always in the ninth

month, always the come-point. How
do I stand this? We become these

words we say, a wailing sound moving
out into the air. These thousands of

worlds that rise from nowhere, how
does your face contain them? I'm

a fly in your honey, then closer, a
moth caught in flame's allure, then

empty sky stretched out in homage.

Underwater in the Fountain

When you die into the soul, you lift
the lid on the cooking pot. You see

the truth of what you've been doing.
It looks sad and terrible before the

crossover move that lets nine levels
of ascension turn into ordinary ground:

silence, conversation with Khidr, blind
and deaf, underwater in the fountain.

Playing and Being Played

There are no words to explain,
no tongue,
                how when that player touches
the strings, it is me playing
and being played,
                how existence turns
around this music, how stories
grow from the trunk,
                how cup and mouth
swallow each other with the wine,
                        how a garnet
stone come from nowhere is puzzled
by these miners,
                how even if you look for us
hair's breadth by hair's breadth, you'll
not find anything. We're inside
the hair!
        How last night a spear struck, how
the lion drips red, how someone pulls
at my robe of tattered patches.
                        "It's all I have!
Where are *your* clothes?"
                How Shams of Tabriz
lives outside time, how what happens
to me happens there.

Friday

For a dervish every day feels like
Friday, the beginning of a holiday,

a fresh setting out that will not have an
end. Dressed in the soul's handsomeness,

you're a whole month of Fridays, sweet
outside, sweet in. Your mind and your deep

being walk together as friends walk along
inside their friendship. Debris does not stay

in one place on a fast-running creek. Let
grudges wash out into the sea. Your soul's

eye watches a spring-green branch moving,
while these other eyes love the old stories.

Drowsy

Drowsy, awake to everything, out
of myself, inside you, the work of

your wine vat where the grapes are
invisible. All one sees is stained

feet tromping about, making a juice
different from ordinary grapes. This

wine gives no hangover. But don't
condemn yourself for living in left-

over stupor. Someone built and set
the hangover trap you find yourself

in! It's the bottom of Joseph's pit,
where he becomes medicine, a clean

tent, a field of stubble and shine.
Shams is winter daylight. I more

resemble the long night coming after.

Continuously

Listening to the prophet David play,
psalms and music, a strange excitement

came, presence *and* patience. Egyptian
granaries full of grain *and* Joseph's

handsomeness. Actual sun *and* nearness.
Sky, undecided; earth, silent: in this

precarious unknowing we live love
doesn't want to say the name of *Hu*.

You stay concealed. A falcon lights.
How far away? Mount Sinai under Moses.

The indications are that you are the one
who appears, not again, but continuously.

An Armor of Roses

Take January's advice. Stack wood.
Weather inevitably turns cold, and you

make fires to stay healthy. Study
the grand metaphor of this yearly work.

Wood is a symbol for *absence*. Fire,
for your love of God. We burn form

to warm the soul. Soul loves winter
for that, and accepts reluctantly the

comfort of spring with its elegant,
proliferating gifts. All part of the

plan: fire becoming ash becoming
garden soil becoming mint, willow, and

tulip. Love looks like fire. Feed
yourself into it. *Be* the fireplace and

the wood. Bravo, for this metallurgy
that makes a needle from an iron ingot.

Calm fire now: for the moth a window;
for you, an armor of roses! Pharaoh

dissolves like yogurt in water. Moses
comes to the top like oil. Fine Arabians

carry royalty. Nags, the sacks of dried
dung. Language is an annoying clatter

in the mill of meaning. A silent river
turns the millstone. The word-grains get

noisily dumped in the tray, pulverized
under the stone as gossip. Let this

poem be thus ground. Let me go
back to the lovefire that refines the

pure gold of my friend, Shamsuddin.

he Pleiades

In absence, aloe wood burns fragrant.
The love we feel is smoke from that.

Existence gets painted with non-existence,
its source, the fire behind a screen.

Smoke born of this fire hides the fire!
Pass through the smoke. Soul, a moving

river; body, the riverbed. Soul can
break the circle of fate and habit.

Take hold the hand of absence and let
it draw you through the Pleiades,

giving up wet and dry, hot and cold.
You become a confidante of Shams Tabriz.

You see clearly the glory of nothing
and stand, inexplicably, there.

Would You Bow?

If the Friend rose inside you, would you
bow? Would you wonder where that one

came from and how? If you say, "I will
bow," that's important. If you answer,

"But can I be sure?" it will keep the
meeting from happening, as busy people

rush there and back here murmuring, *Now
I know; no, I don't know now.* Have you

seen a camel with its eyes covered turn
and walk one way, then turn another?

Be silent and revolve with no will.
Don't raise your hand to ask anything.

Holy one, sitting in the body's well
like Joseph, a rope is there in front

of you. Lift your hand to that! A
blind man has bought you for eighteen

counterfeit coins. Empty metal cups
bang together, and the full moon slides

out of hiding. Make one sound, please!
You are the precious hyacinth that the

sickle will spare, not the wheat plant
Adam ate. I remind you with these poems

to dress in the flower of God's qualities,
not your torn robe of self-accusation.

Ashes, Wanderers

In this battle we do not hold
a shield in front of us. When

we turn in *sama*, we do not hear
the flute or the tambourine.

Underneath these feet we become
nazar, the guide's glance, ashes,

wanderers: as the moon diminishes
every day and then it's gone, to

come back changed. Send for the
planet Venus to play here! Flute,

drum, and strings are not enough.
No. Who but *these* musicians could

stand the heat that melts the sun?

The Day's Great Wooden Bowl

Still dizzy from last night's
wine? Wait a while. Don't reach

yet for this we serve. You can't
really be on the ocean with scenes

of familiar creeks and your loved
home-river in your eyes. Wait,

if you're caught in memory. As
those with business ideas were

driven from the temple courtyard,
so bitter, self-important people

need to be excluded from the mix
being stirred in this day's great

wooden bowl. In the room with
the Chinese princess, popular

songs fade. Don't boil the hard
unripened grapes, and don't sell

vinegar! This moment is the perfect
grape you crush to make your life-

wine interesting. You might, in
such a moment, meet someone as

I met Shams. God knows what
orchard you'll be walking then!

So We Can Have What We Want

Your wear coarse wool, but you're a king,
as the soul's energy hides, as love

remembers. You enter this room in a human
shape *and* as the atmosphere we breathe.

You are the central pole through the nine
levels connecting them and us to absolute

absence. So that we can have what we want,
you give failure and frustration. You want

only the company of the lion and the lion
cub, no wobbly legs. That man there, you

suggest, might remove his head before
entering the temple. Then he could listen

without ears to a voice that says, *My
creature.* A month of walking the road, you

make that distance in one day. Never mind
gold and silver payments. When you feel

generous, give your head. My beauty,
you have no need for a guide. The one

who follows and the one who leads are
inseparable, as the moon and the circle

around it. An Arab drags his camel town
to town. You go through your troubles and

changing beliefs, both no different from
the moon moving across or basil growing

and getting cut for a bouquet. It doesn't
matter you've been lost. The hoopoe is

still looking for you. It's another
beginning, my friend, this waking in a

morning with no haze, and help coming
without your asking! A glass submerged

is turning inside the wine. With grief
waved away, sweet gratefulness arrives.

Entering the Shell

Love is *alive*, and someone borne
along by it is *more* alive than lions

roaring or men in their fierce courage.
Bandits ambush others on the road.

They get wealth, but they stay in one
place. Lovers keep moving, never

the same, not for a second! What
makes others grieve, they enjoy!

When they look angry, don't believe
their faces. It's spring lightning,

a joke before the rain. They chew
thorns thoughtfully along with pasture

grass. Gazelle and lioness, having
dinner. Love is invisible except

here, in us. Sometimes I praise love;
sometimes love praises me. Love,

a little shell somewhere on the ocean
floor, opens its mouth. *You* and *I*

and *we*, those imaginary beings, enter
that shell as a single sip of seawater.

You Are As You Are

Yesterday, you made a promise.
Today, you broke it. Yesterday,

Bistami's dance. Today, dregs
thrown out. In pieces, and at

the same time, a perfect glass
filled with sunlight. Give up

on figuring the appearances, the
dressing in green like a Sufi.

You don't resemble anyone. You're
not the bride or the groom. You

don't fit in a house with a family.
You've left the closed-in corner

where you lived. Domestic animals
get ridden to work. Not you. You

are as you are, an indescribable
message coming on the air. Every

word you say, medicine. But
not yet: stay quiet and still.

Birds Nesting near the Coast

Soul, if you want to learn secrets,
your heart must forget about shame

and dignity. You are God's lover,
yet you worry what people are saying.

The rope belt the early Christians
wore to show who they were, throw

it away! Inside, you are sweet
beyond telling, and the cathedral

there, so deeply tall. Evening now,
more your desire than a woman's hair.

And not knowledge: walk with those
innocent of that: faces inside fire,

birds nesting near the coast, earning
their beauty, servants to the ocean.

There is a sun within every person,
the *you* we call companion.

As Lakewater Rises in Mist

The singer sings about love, until
the Friend appears in the doorway.

Kitchen smoke drifts up into clouds
and becomes a thousand-year-old wine.

I am here, not reckoning the credit
accumulated or future speculation.

I am the vineyard and the barrel
where the grapes are crushed, the

entire operation, whose transaction
pours this glass of wine, this moment,

this poem. A man stumbles by with
baggage, papers from the house, regret

and wishing, not knowing which to
tend to. Neither. After you see

the face, concerns change, as
lakewater rises into mist.

More Is Required

You've disappeared into the way?
Leave even that behind. Sit

with the essence inside love.
In that Chinese mirror you'll see

hundreds of sword blades. Don't
be afraid to use them. You've

given up everything. You live
in absence. More is required.

Mix an eye medicine with the ground.
Sweep the memory-pictures clean.

Swing down and cut. A voice
comes in the broken place. Pull

the tree-wing up by its roots.
Love wants an arm and a leg.

Two Days of Silence

This wonderful moment, the taste of
nothing, in the company of the poor

and the empty. Sit with Bistami, not
some fortune teller. There are more

than two holidays a year! We celebrate
a birthday and a solstice every second.

Newborns, we need fresh bread! Life
grows from the dead, as the living get

led into death. Dry branches to the
fire: green limbs bend to the ground with

fruit; pleasure fills a mother's breast:
put your mouth there and suck. You

must. I've made many elegant speeches
to the assembly. Now it's time to

walk outside and be quiet. Shams draws
me to words, then two days of silence.

Your Morning Shade

You are the dawn that arrives in
the middle of the night, dark hair-

strands of music filling the reed,
understanding entering through ear

and eye, the fragrant steam of soup.
Signs and specific instructions

articulate from you, teaching us new
ways to wander. Asking *why* and *how*

is no longer right. Say soul is like
the feet of an ant, or oceanwater,

bitter and salty, or a snake that has
the antidote for its poison also in its

skull: we push through these puzzling
forms to sit in your morning shade.

What's Not Here

I start out on this road, call it
love or *emptiness*. I only know what's

not here: resentment seeds, back-
scratching greed, worrying about out-

come, fear of people. When a bird gets
free, it doesn't go back for remnants

left on the bottom of the cage! Close
by, I'm rain. Far off, a cloud of fire.

I seem restless, but I am deeply at ease.
Branches tremble; the roots are still.

I am a universe in a handful of dirt,
whole when totally demolished. Talk

about *choices* does not apply to me.
While intelligence considers options,

I am somewhere lost in the wind.

*Inside the Rose

That camel there with its calf running
behind it, Sutur and Koshek, we're like

them: mothered and nursed by where and
who we are from, following our fates

where they lead, until we hear a drum
begin, grace entering our lives, a prayer

of gratitude. We feel the call of God,
and the journey changes. A dry field

of stones turns soft and moist as cheese.
The mountain feels level under us. Love

becomes agile and quick, and suddenly
we're there! This traveling's not done

with the body. God's secret takes form
in *your loving*. But there *are* those in

bodies who are pure soul. It can happen.
These messengers invite us to walk with

them. They say, "You may feel happy
enough where you are, but we can't do

without you any longer! Please." So
we walk along inside the rose, being

pulled like the creeks and rivers are,
out from the town onto the plain. My

guide, my soul, your only sadness is when
I am not walking with you. In deep silence,

with *some* exertion to stay in your company,
I could save you a lot of trouble!

A Walking Fire

Today, now, this is when
we can meet the Friend,

now, as the sun comes up.
The Beloved, who yesterday

was so distant, today is
kind and bringing food.

Someone who knows this
one and isn't demolished

completely and reborn, that
someone is made of marble,

not blood and bone and brain
and eyes and hair. Gabriel

knocks on the Friend's door.
"Who is it?" "Your servant."

"Who came with you?" "Your
love." "Where?" "In my

arms." "But the whole world
is in love with me. What

you've brought is a common
thing. Go away." Now Shams

comes along, a walking fire
beyond anything I can say.

The Knots Untie

Fire is whispering a secret in smoke's
ear, "This aloe wood loves me because

I help it live out its purpose. With
me it becomes fragrance, and then

disappears altogether!" The knots
untie and open into absence, as you do

with me, my friend. Eaten by flame,
and smoked out into the sky! This is

most fortunate. What's unlucky is *not*
to change and disappear. The black soil

must crumble to give itself to plants.
Think how sperm and egg become a smiling

face and head. Bread must dissolve to
turn into thought. Gold and silver in

their raw forms aren't worth much. This
way leads through humiliation and contempt.

We've tried the fullness of presence. Now
it's time for desolation. Love is pulling

us out by the ears to school. Love wants
us clean of resentment and those impulses

that misguide our souls. We're asleep,
but Khidr keeps sprinkling water on our

faces. Love will tell us the rest of
what we need to know soon. Then we'll

be deeply asleep and profoundly awake
simultaneously like cave companions.

The Shine in the Fields

The shine in the fields and in the orchard
has become the light of your face. No

home now, no loved occupation, no belongings,
no figuring profit and loss. When this

love comes, it's impossible to worry about
honor or reputation, what the community

gives, the more and the less. There's no
longer any demarcation line between "the

worlds." Hats fly off. A pack of dogs snarl
and bite each other around a carcass. We're

not those dogs. Only God knows our secrets,
and that's enough. We have no more discussions

about God or arguments over doctrine. What
is planted in each person's soul will sprout.

We surrender to however that happens.
Companions used to be magnets that drew us

together to talk. No more. No more even
the sun! It has turned itself into the face

of Shams-i Tabriz, the sanctity and praise.

I Am Not This

I am not this. Your beauty closes
my eyes, and I am falling into

that. You cut the umbilical with
this love that's been with me since

birth. My mother saw your mountain
reflected in my face, you that lift

coverings, you that bring death. We
agreed on this before creation. I've

been so hidden. Ask my body who I
am. It says *solid ground*. Ask my

soul. *Dizzy as the wind*. Neither,
I stand here facing Shams of Tabriz.

Fierce Courtesy

The connection to the Friend
is secret and very fragile.

The image of that friendship
is in how *you* love, the grace

and delicacy, the subtle talking
together, in full prostration,

outside of time. When you're
there, remember the fierce

courtesy of the one with you.

A Smile and a Gentleness

There is a smile and a gentleness
inside. When I learned the name

and address of that, I went to where
you sell perfume. I begged you not

to trouble me so with longing. Come
out and play! Flirt more naturally.

Teach me how to kiss. On the ground
a spread blanket, flame that's caught

and burning well, cumin seeds browning,
I am inside all this with my soul.

Out in Empty Sky

If you catch a fragrance of the unseen,
like that, you won't be able to be

contained. You'll be out in empty sky.
Any beauty the world has, any desire,

will easily be yours. As you live
deeper in the heart, the mirror gets

clearer and cleaner. Shams of Tabriz
realized God in himself. When that

happens, you have no anxieties about
losing anyone or anything. You break

the spells human difficulties cause.
Interpretations come, hundreds, from

all the religious symbols and parables
and prayers. You know what they mean,

when God lives through you like Shams.

*W*ooden Walking Stick

Friend, you are Moses. I the wooden
walking stick. Sometimes that simple use.

Other times, a dragon earth-energy. You
decide. There's no time or place in the air

you inhabit. The days you give me I give
back to you. I have seen your unseeable

beauty and taken report without words to
my heart, which became all eye with the news.

"Long life to eyes," says my heart now over
and over. Hundreds of candles search the

turning sky. No bread in the basket, no
money; home, family, work, in shambles, with

your light shining on the ruin. Crushed
in grief's mortar, let me be medicine for

other eyes. What is the soul? Half a leaf.
What is the heart? A flower opening. I am

not the one speaking here. Even so, I'll
stop. Anything anyone says is your voice.

A World Dense with Greeting

The soul comes every day at dawn. "Good
to see you again, my friend. The peace

of God be with you." No matter where
you are or what you're doing, talking,

silent, asleep, soul comes and greets
you like that. Your soul sees your

purity. Body sees your pretensions and
deceit. You are a rose that heals

woundedness. "Hello again," call out
the thorns. I go to the village chief.

I say, "God be with you." He gives me
a glass of wine. "Hold this carefully.

Keep it safe." "The peace of God," I tell
him. "But did you know that I am crazy?

I like to sit in the fire with Abraham."
Then I turn and thank God. *Salaam*

Aleichem. I walk out. The world is
dense with greeting. I respond in kind,

then back into the cave with my Beloved.
Subtle artwork appears everywhere. *It's*

so fine to be with you. David from
the throne agrees to be thrown down!

Hallaj nods *namaste* from the cross. One
who is longing for your praise waves

without expecting anything. Someone
deeply in need signals helplessly.

The king puts up an appropriate banner.
The sick mouthe "Hey." I undress and walk

toward whatever's next. Every string
on the instrument sings *salaam* to

every other. Death brings good health.
I let words loose like mountain runoff,

read Sura 61, which warns of finding
images for what has no likeness, and

leave the job I imagined for myself with
one thought, *God bless. Adios, do svi-*

danye, toodle-oo, au revoir, ciao, aloha,
teshekkür ederim, may your well run deep.

Spring Murmur

Young, loving, springlike, these qualities
come up in many combinations.
                                        Watch
the fields,
            the garden,
                        the forest,
how they change in time.
                            Their prayer in winter,
No God but you. Their prayer in spring,
the same, both asking for help.
                                Listen now
to the murmur of their conversation:
                                        branch with fruit,
"I'm about to break!"
                        "That's funny," says the tulip.
Narcissus looks love at jasmine. Iris jabbering,
"Now don't be bitter." Violet kneels, pretending.
Waterlily knows everything.
                                Hyacinth wags her head.
Mint turns to stare at grass running everywhere
barefooted. Bud hides. Willow drags
a watery arm in the mirror
of the river.
                Dove keeps the query going; "Where . . .
where . . . have you been . . . where?"
                                        Partridge: "No where."
Falcon; "What brought you here
                        from there?"
                                        Look around.
These are just a fraction of who might be
                                    wandering in.
See now:
            fig, pomegranate,
                        October apple, orange,

and finally, grapes.

They like to walk slow,

the first

coming last, sweet and stringent like

the mind,

that trusts and also doubts.

Melon arrives in a house

with no door, as pumpkin, broken open,

fills with rain.

We argue about food. We want what we

want. These gorgeous details fascinate

like a Chinese painting, soul

being the artist.

That's what I used to call Shams,

the great Chinese screen painter!

Everyone Outdoors Talking

First day of spring,
beginning a whole year of spring!

Everyone outdoors talking.
                              Rose to narcissus:
"Have you seen that ugly raven's face?"
                                        "No, he has no
interest in us."
                "That's good news!"
                                    Pomegranate
asks the apple tree for a peach.
                              "All you loafers
down at that end of the orchard, you're
always wanting peaches."
                        "You got to have a soul like *Jesus*
to be handed a peach!"
                      Inside this ordinary banter
come messages from the source,
from absolute absence.
                      The plants stretch new wings
in the sun. Cloud and fog burn off.
                                    "Bless your heart."
"That's enough."
                Sun moves into Aries, permanently!
                                              "Come
see me."
        "I will."
              "I'd like that."
                              "But I can't leave this."
Ground soaked, sky
                  full of candles.
                                  Visions of fire
and water alternating.
                      Drag your feet off the boat.
Look at him standing there.

I used to have mountain
ranges inside my chest. Now it's smooth plain.

Grief lives between the cat paws.
You can say *eek-eek* or *gehk-gohk*,
but there's no way to escape.

Throw this cloth-making equipment into the fire,
the alphabet spindle that's stuck in your throat,
the cleft stick of your neck wrapped with thread.

Daring Enough to Finish

Face that lights my face, you spin
intelligence into these particles

I am. Your wind shivers my tree.
My mouth tastes sweet with your name

in it. You make my dance daring enough
to *finish*. No more timidity! Let

fruit fall and wind turn my roots up
in the air, done with patient waiting.

What I See in Your Eyes

Out of myself, but wanting to go
beyond that, wanting what I see

in your eyes, not power, but to
kiss the ground with the dawn

breeze for company, wearing white
pilgrim cloth. I have a certain

knowing. Now I want sight.

Music Is My Zikr

As the hoopoe loves to hear
Solomon's whistle, I want the reed flute
and the harp, the *rebab* and drum,
burning in the mode of *Ispahan* . . .
then *Hicaz* . . .

        Take a chord from *Irak* . . .

                with some

Uzzak . . .

     to *Rast* . . .

          the wail of *Buselik* . . .

               Now slip

into *Huseyni* . . .

        Maye . . .

            the vast and tiny melodies
singing me to sleep.

         Rehavi . . .

            to wake with *Zengule* . . .

Music is my *zikr*.
These names are all I know.
Let the mind's other concerns go.

This love is more subtle,

           as wind through a field
stirs wildflower scent,

          by music-light fresh beauties
appear: that's all I want.

More of Your Names

To say more of your names: you
are the one who was with us

at the beginning, telling secrets
in the first house. We were

afraid of fire, but then we found
your flame. You are also a wind

that puts out the mind's candle,
that city leveled. With friends,

friendship. With enemies, the
standing apart, or right in

the middle, resembling both.
Knowledgeable ones sigh their

disdain: "Oh the stories lovers
tell!" But you *are* those stories,

you that bring dawn to the end of
night. Beauty that originates,

the look and the presence inside
the look, majesty of Shamsuddin,

praise and the light-connecting
ligaments that hold this earth.

Even Better

With three strings play the mode
of *Rehavi* . . .
                    Sing us into union,
no more ambivalence.
                              If you don't have
zir or *bem*, the high and the low
strings on the lute,
                    even better.
Now grief comes over with a *Neva* song . . .
                                        Sing

our lack of songs. You go away
on the *Irak* mode . . .
                        draw near stroking *Ispahan* . . .
Wild with *Zengule* . . .
                        finishing the matter, but still
we're nervous and dull.
                    This music
is and is not.
              A stretch of *Rast* . . .
                              reaches into
Hicaz . . .
        Juseyni into *Ussak* . . .
                              and on to the pure
joy of *Buselik* and *Maye* . . .
                        We ask for *Dugah* . . .
You give *Cargah* . . .
                    Candle, sunlight over countryside,
I call you a changing beauty
that sings and blesses this place with every mode.

Thorn Witness

Apparent shapes and meanings change.
Creature hunts down creature. Bales

get unloaded and weighed to determine
price. None of any of this pertains

to the unseen fire we call the Beloved.
That presence has no form, and cannot

be understood or measured. Take
your hands away from your face. If

a wall of dust moves across the plain,
there's usually an army advancing

under it. When you look for the Friend,
the Friend is looking for you. Carried

by a strong current, you and the others
with you seem to be making decisions,

but you're not. I weave coarse wool.
I decide to talk less. But my actions

cause nothing. A thorn grows next to
the rose as its witness. I am that

thorn for whom simply to *be* is an act
of praise. Near the rose, no shame.

Transparent Tree

I've traded my soul for the universe.
Don't speak. The jeweler who thought

he was buying gold to work with now
owns the mine! But commerce metaphors

are wrong. What has happened in me
is more profound, like a fish under-

water beginning to say words! A
transparent tree grows in the night-sky

orchard where I have found a little
corner to be in, as when two planets

intersect. I have met Shams.

The Self We Share

Thirst is angry at water. Hunger, bitter
with bread. The cave wants nothing to do

with the sun. This is dumb, the self-
defeating way we've been. A gold mine is

calling us into its temple. Instead, we
bend and keep picking up rocks from the

ground. Every *thing* has a shine like gold,
but we should turn to the source! The

origin is what we truly are. I add a little
vinegar to the honey I give. The bite of

scolding makes ecstasy more familiar. But
look, fish, you're already in the ocean:

just swimming there makes you friends with
glory. What are these grudges about? You

are Benjamin. Joseph has put a gold cup
in your grain sack and accused you of being

a thief. Now he draws you aside and says,
"You are my brother. I am a prayer. You're

the *amen*." We move in eternal regions, yet
worry about property here. This is the

prayer of each: *You are the source of my
life. You separate essence from mud. You*

honor my soul. You bring rivers from the
mountain springs. You brighten my eyes. The

wine you offer takes me out of myself into
the self we share. Doing that is religion.

 Hoofbeats

The sound of hoofbeats leaving a monastery
where all is timed and measured: you are

that rider: someone who does not care very
much about *things* and results, illness or

loss: you are the soul inside the soul
that's always traveling. Mind gathers

bait. The personality carries a grudge.
You weave cloth like the moon leaving

no trace on the road. There's a learning
community where the names of God are talked

about and memorized, and there's another
residence where meanings *live*. You're on

your way from here to there, and don't claim
you're not carrying gifts! Your graceful

manner gives color and fragrance, as creekwater
animates landscape it moves through. Hundreds

of caravans sail into the sky. You travel alone,
by yourself, those caravans: sun inside one

dazzling mote, the emperor's serenity on night-
watch as alert as his palace guard. You enchant

this visible place, so that we imagine you're
going somewhere, off to new country! The absolute

unknowable appears as spring and disappears in
fall. Signs come, not the essence signified.

How long will you be a shepherd single-filing
us in and out of the human barn? Will I ever

see you as you secretly are in silence?

Raw, Well-Cooked, Burnt

You ask, "Why do you cry with such
sweetness all around?" I weep as I

make the honey, wearing the shirt
of a bee, and I refuse to share this

suffering. I play the sky's harp. I
curl around my treasure like a snake.

You say, "What is this 'I' business?"
Friend, I've been a long time away

from that. What you see here is
your own reflection. I am still raw,

and at the same time well-cooked, and
burnt to a crisp! No one can tell if

I'm laughing or weeping. I wonder myself.
How can I be separated and yet in union?

Both Worlds

There is God's wine, and this
other. Don't mix them. There

are naked pilgrims who wear only
sunlight. Don't give them clothes!

There are lovers content with
hoping. I'm not one of them.

Give a cup of pure fire to your
closest friend, healing salve

to the wounded. To Shams-i
Tabriz, offer up both worlds.

God in the Stew

Is there a human mouth that doesn't
give out soul-sound? Is there love,

a drawing-together of any kind, that
isn't sacred? Every natural dog

sniffs God in the stew. The lion's
paw trembles like a rose petal.

He senses the ultimate spear coming.
In the shepherd's majesty wolves

and lambs tease each other. Look
inside your mind. Do you hear

the crowd gathering? Help coming,
every second. Still you cover

your eyes with mud. Watch the horned
owl. Wash your face. Anyone who

steps into an orchard walks inside
the orchard keeper. Millions of

love-tents bloom on the plain. A
star in your chest says, *None*

of this is outside you. Close your
lips and let the maker of mouths

talk, the one who says *things*.

Undressing

Learn the alchemy true human beings
know: the moment you accept what

troubles you've been given, the door
will open. Welcome difficulty

as a familiar comrade. Joke with
torment brought by the Friend.

Sorrows are the rags of old clothes
and jackets that serve to cover,

then are taken off. That undressing,
and the naked body underneath, is

the sweetness that comes after grief.

Silkworms

The hurt you embrace becomes joy.
Call it to your arms where it can

change. A silkworm eating leaves
makes a cocoon. Each of us weaves

a chamber of leaves and sticks.
Silkworms begin to truly exist

as they disappear inside that room.
Without legs, we fly. When I stop

speaking, this poem will close,
and open its silent wings . . .

Musk in a Small Box

Two things impossible: to fill a saddlebag
with air, and to make a lover of God repent.

If guilt and atonement were an ocean, I would
not be wet. If I were buried in the ground,

dirt would start smoking and catch fire.
Particles keep turning, and my soul keeps

imagining and desiring. That's its work, my
livelihood. A saddlemaker rides to another

town, but he still makes saddles. Everything
alive goes to the grave. Be a slave to

the ground! Musk in a small box stays musky.
Whenever your heart grows light inside your

chest, your chest is not a dungeon, but a sky,
a great pasture. Babies get very happy in

the womb. Blood is better than wine for them.
The smallness, a rose garden. I hesitate to

say this because it might be misunderstood.

Why and Where We Go

You are more beautiful than soul,
more useful than eyes; whatever I've

seen in myself, I didn't see it.
You saw. You chose me. I say this

poem to honor that choice. I chose
to lie down in a burning coffin-bed!

Ask my eyes, "Why do you flow?" Ask
my back, "Why so bent?" Ask my soul,

"Why do you wear iron shoes on the road?"
Also ask my soul if it has met another

like you, or heard of such a thing in
any language. You're the sun dissolving

dull overcast, the fragrance of a field,
Joseph entering *this* room. Peeling

oranges, we see you and nick our hands.
Without touching the ground, you draw

a line. We turn that way. You're why
and where we go, and what we do there.

A Voice Through the Door

Sometimes you hear a voice through
the door calling you, as fish out of

water hear the waves, or a hunting
falcon hears the drum's *come back*.

This turning toward what you deeply
love saves you. Children fill their

shirts with rocks and carry them
around. We're not children anymore.

Read the book of your life which has
been given you. A voice comes to

your soul saying, *Lift your foot;*
cross over; move into the emptiness

of question and answer and question.

Solomon Ant

This feverish desiring does not calm
down, because God doesn't want it to.

Wishes and wantings come from there.
When my shirt is wet, blame the sea!

We soul-fish swim among the fishing
lines of what we want, unable to imagine

the beauty of the fisherpeople jiggling
the hooks! God was here before the

universe. What *desire* brought us into
being? I do not know. It's enough that

we go straight for what and who we are
drawn to. No. There's no crooked or

straight with this, though we persist in
judging actions and their source: bad,

bad, bad, good, good. Think of an ant
that wants to fly. Wonderful! He digs at

the palace wall. He claims to be Solomon.
He demands a crown. This is how we are.

We are not what we're wanting, and yet
somehow the longings are not apart from

us. Shams, will you untie this knot?

As Fish Drink the Ocean

This world eats men and women; we become
ground, and yet God sends us here to eat

the whole universe. Earth tries to work
a sorcery on us saying *tomorrow, tomorrow,*

but we outwit that spell by enjoying this
now. Say we were born from invisible beings

that gather in the middle of the night. Say
that's why we love the night so. We love,

and taste the wine of being human, as fish
drink the ocean. Do you think that alters

the sea? Sea and see: how one values the
Beloved depends on the state of the lover.

What are *you* worth! Which candle draws you
to die in *its* light? Shams of Tabriz is the act

of seeing, one who looks and the sun itself.
There is no way to understand such a presence.

What Is the Heart?

What is the heart? It is not human,
and it is not imaginary. I call it

you. Stately bird, who one moment
combines with this world, and the

next, passes through the boundary to
the unseen. The soul cannot find you

because you are the soul's wings, how
it moves. Eyes cannot see you: you

are the source of sight. You're the
one thing repentance will not repent,

nor news report. Spring comes: one
seed refuses to germinate and start

being a tree. One poor piece of wood
blackens but will not catch fire.

The alchemist wonders at a bit of
copper that resists turning to gold.

Who am I that I'm with you and still
myself? When the sun comes up,

the complicated nightmind of the
constellations fades. Snowforms do

not last through July. The heart-
quality embodied by our master, Shams

Tabriz, will always dissolve the old
quarrel between those who believe in

the dignity of a human being's decisions
and those who claim they're all illusion.

Great Rose Tree

This is the day and the year
of the rose. The whole garden

is opening with laughter. Iris
whispering to cypress. The rose

is the joy of meeting someone.
The rose is a world imagination

cannot imagine. A messenger from
the orchard where the soul lives.

A small seed that points to a great
rose *tree*! Hold its hand and walk

like a child. A rose is what grows
from the work the prophets do.

Full moon, new moon. Accept the
invitation spring extends, four

birds flying toward a master. A rose
is all these, and the silence that

closes and sits in the shade, a bud.

ord Fog

Words, even if they come from
the soul, hide the soul, as fog

rising off the sea covers the sea,
the coast, the fish, the pearls.

It's noble work to build coherent
philosophical discourses, but

they block out the sun of truth.
See God's qualities as an ocean,

this world as foam on the purity
of that. Brush away and look

through the alphabet to essence,
as you do the hair covering your

beloved's eyes. Here's the mystery:
this intricate, astonishing world

is proof of God's presence even as
it covers the beauty. One flake

from the wall of a gold mine does
not give much idea what it's like

when the sun shines in and turns
the air and the workers golden.

Stranded Somewhere

If you are the body, that one is the soul
of the universe. If you're soul, that

one is the soul within all souls. Wherever
you go, whatever you are, listen for the

voice that asks, "Who will be sacrificed
tonight?" Jump up and volunteer! Accept

this cup that is offered every second.
Love has written the thousand subtleties

of this call on my face. Read. If you're
bored and contemptuous, love is a walk in

a meadow. If you're stranded somewhere
and exhausted, love is an Arabian horse.

The ocean feeds *itself* to its fish. If
you're ocean fish, why bother with bread

the ground grows? These jars of grief and
trouble we call bodies, throw stones and

break them! My cage is this longing for
Shams. Be my worst enemy: shatter it!

Too Vast for Partnership

Will it be better for us when we
dissolve into the ground, or worse?

Let's learn now what will happen.
This is lovers' work, to break through

and become this earth, *to die before
we die.* Don't think of pairing up

somehow with God! That claim is a
religious self-indulgence. You know

it by the smell: smoke coming off
dried dung is different from that of

aloe wood! The presence that one
second is soil, then water, fire,

smoke, woof, warp, a friend, a shame,
a modesty, is too vast and intimate

for partnership! *Observers* watch as
presence takes thousands of forms.

But *inside* your eyes the presence
does not brighten or dim; it just

lives there. A saint or a prophet,
one like Muhammad can *see* the trees

of heaven, the fruit hanging so close
he could reach and pick one for his

friend. But it's not time for that.
They melt and flow away from sight.

What Have You Been Drinking?

I'm drifting off to sleep; you wake
me up wanting new musical words, new

languagelike flute notes. My hands
and feet are dormant; you pull my ear.

Tell the story again from the beginning.
Dark strands of evening cover the earth.

You beg for poems about night's hair,
how sweetness rises in the canebrake.

I finish one poem. You want another,
another. Imagine this: you're dead

tired, ready for sleep. Your assistant
comes wanting to hear about *ambergris*!

What would you do? What have you been
drinking that you want so many ecstatic

poems? These are not real questions.
I'm joking. In your presence, call me

any name, *Kaymaz, Sencer*; all the same,
particle underfoot, floating dustmote.

Fastened to a Pole

I keep turning around this misfortune,
this troubled illusion I call myself,

when I could be turning around *you*,
the giver of blessings, origin and

presence. My chest is a grave you
made a rose garden. What goes in the

grave? What fits in that two-by-two-
by-seven? Not soul, soul cannot be

contained by the sky! I turn around
God. I have become a mirror, yet I

turn for these few days around a piece
of white wool. If I were a rose in

this spring, I would change into a
hundred rose bushes. I turn around this

frustrated body, tethered in a barn
of words, when I could be free in the

infinite pasture. Free, why do I keep
turning as though fastened to a pole?

Saladin

Heart sees the joy of early dawn,
the breeze. What have you seen?

What have you not seen? Sometimes,
to plunge in a bewilderment ocean;

sometimes, to find the gray amber
of whales deep in the mountain!

Hundreds of windows. Haze returns
into the sea. My weeping eyes,

wave by wave, mix with the ocean.
It becomes an eye. Both worlds,

a single corn grain in front of a
great rooster! One who wants, one

who is wanted, the same. Who knows
God? Someone through with *La*. No!

The broken lover knows about this.
Nobody in this robe but God. Appear

as you truly are. Saladin, you are
my soul, the eye that sees God.

Ready for Silence

The devotional moon looks into
the heart and *is in* the heart.

When the heart has a Friend like
you, the universe cannot contain

their pleasure. Anyone warmed
by sun feels courage coming in.

If grief arrives, you enjoy it.
Generosity: that's your hand in

my pocket giving your wealth away.
Yet you run from me like one

raised in the wild. Here comes
this strange creature: me, in a

hands-and-feet shape! The formless
tries to satisfy us with forms!

A transparent nakedness wearing
pure light says, *Blessed are those*

who put on gold brocade! You may
not see him, but Moses is alive,

in this town, and he still has his
staff! And there's water and thirst,

wherever and however water goes, and
the one who brings water. The morning

wind broke off a few branches in the
garden. No matter. When you feel

love inside you, you hear the
invitation to be cooked by God.

It's that creation the heart loves.
For three winter months the ground

keeps quiet. But each piece of earth
knows what's inside waiting: beans,

sugarcane, cypress, wildflowers. Then
the spring sun comes talking plants

into the open. Anyone who feels the
point of prayer bends down like

the first letter of *pray*. Anyone who
walks with his back to the sun is

following his shadow. Move into your
own quietness. This word-search poem

has found *you*, ready for silence.

A Man Talking to His House

I say that no one in this caravan is awake
and that while you sleep, a thief is stealing

the signs and symbols of what you thought
was your life. Now you're angry with me for

telling you this! Pay attention to those who
hurt your feelings telling you the truth.

Giving and absorbing compliments is like
trying to paint on water, that insubstantial.

Here is how a man once talked with his house.
"Please, if you're ever about to collapse,

let me know." One night without a word the
house fell. "What happened to our agreement?"

The house answered, "Day and night I've been
telling you with cracks and broken boards and

holes appearing like mouths opening. But you
kept patching and filling those with mud, so

proud of your stopgap masonry. You didn't
listen." This house is your body always

saying, *I'm leaving; I'm going soon.* Don't
hide from one who knows the secret. Drink

the wine of turning toward God. Don't examine
your urine. Examine instead how you praise,

what you wish for, this longing we've been
given. Fall turns pale light yellow wanting

spring, and spring arrives! Seeds blossom.
Come to the orchard and see what comes to

you, a silent conversation with your soul.

Every Tree

Every tree, every growing thing as it
grows, says this truth: *You harvest what*

you sow. With life as short as a half-
taken breath, don't plant anything but

love. The value of a human being can
be measured by what he or she most deeply

wants. Be free of possessing things.
Sit at an empty table. Be pleased with

water, the taste of being home. People
travel the world looking for the Friend,

but that one is always at home! Jesus
moves quickly to Mary. A donkey stops

to smell the urine of another donkey.
There are simple reasons for what happens:

you won't stay clear for long if you sit
with the one who pours wine. Someone

with a cup of honey in hand rarely has
a sour face. If someone says a eulogy,

there must be a funeral nearby. A rose
opens because she *is* the fragrance she

loves. We speak poems, and lovers down
the centuries will keep saying them.

The cloth God weaves doesn't wear out.

I Met One Traveling

In the evening between sleep and awakening,
I met one traveling. He was the light of

consciousness. His body was soul, his pure
wisdom apparent in his beautiful face. He

praises me for a while, then scolds, "You
sit on the seven-sky throne, in prison.

The sign of Gemini has set a table for you,
yet you stick your head down a drainhole

again. Essence is not nourished with food
and sleep. Do no one any harm in this

timefield of short crops, where what you
sow comes back up very quickly! You try to

accomplish things, to win, to reach goals.
This is not the true situation. Put the

whole world in ambition's stomach, it'll
never be enough. Assume you get everything

you want. Assume you have it now. What's
the point? The next moment, you die.

Friend, the youth you've lived is ending.
You sleep a drunken dreamless sleep with no

sense what morning you could wake inside."

Autumn Rose Elegy

You've gone to the secret world.
Which way is it? You broke the cage

and flew. You heard the drum that
calls you home. You left this hu-

miliating shelf, this disorienting
desert where we're given wrong

directions. What use now a crown?
You've become the sun. No need for

a belt: you've slipped out of your
waist! I have heard that near the

end you were eyes looking at soul.
No looking now. You live inside

the soul. You're the strange autumn
rose that led the winter wind in

by withering. You're rain soaking
everywhere from cloud to ground. No

bother of talking. Flowing silence
and sweet sleep beside the Friend.

The Bright Core of Failure

Sometimes you enter the heart. Sometimes
you're born from the soul. Sometimes you

weep a song of separation: all the same
glory. You live in beautiful forms and

you're the energy that breaks images. All
light, neither this nor that. Human beings

go places on foot; angels, with wings. Even
if they find nothing but ruins and failure,

you're the bright core of that. When angels
and humans are free of feet and wings, they'll

understand that you are that lack, pure
absence. You're in my eyes like a taste of

wine that blocks my understanding. That
ignorance glorifies. You talk and feel in

the talking: kingdom, finances, fire, smoke,
the senses, incense: all are your favorites!

A ship, Noah, blessings, luck, troubles that
pull us unknowingly toward treasure: look,

he's being dragged away from his friends!
Nobody will see him anymore. This is your

story. I ask you, "Should I talk to this one?
Is he being drawn to me?" Silence. That too.

What is desire? What is it! Don't laugh, my
soul. Show me the way through this desiring.

All the world loves you, but you are nowhere
to be found. Hidden and completely obvious.

You are the soul! You boil me down in a
saucepan, then ask why I'm spilling out. Is

it time for patience? Your bright being. My
heart is a saucepan. This writing, the record

of being torn apart in your fire, as aloe
wood most becomes itself when burning up.

Enough *talk about* burning! Everything, even
the end of this poem, is a taste of your glory.

Listening

What is the deep listening? *Sama* is
a greeting from the secret ones inside

the heart, a letter. The branches of
your intelligence grow new leaves in

the wind of this listening. The body
reaches a peace. Rooster sound comes,

reminding you of your love for dawn.
The reed flute and the singer's lips:

the knack of how spirit breathes into
us becomes as simple and ordinary as

eating and drinking. The dead rise with
the pleasure of listening. If someone

can't hear a trumpet melody, sprinkle
dirt on his head and declare him dead.

Listen, and feel the beauty of your
separation, the unsayable absence.

There's a moon inside every human being.
Learn to be companions with it. Give

more of your life to this listening. As
brightness is to time, so you are to

the one who talks to the deep ear in
your chest. I should sell my tongue

and buy a thousand ears when that
one steps near and begins to speak.

NOTES

A General Introductory Lecture, line 3. Hallaj was the tenth-century Sufi martyr killed for saying *I am the Truth*.

Hamza's Nothing. Hamza was Rumi's flute player.

Underwater in the Fountain, line 7. Khidr is a mysterious prophet-saint whose actions, as described in the Qur'an (18:65–82), are incomprehensible to Moses. When Moses protests Khidr's seemingly immoral actions, Khidr explains what motivated them: a caring for other people that goes beyond the more visible virtue Moses had expected.

Continuously, line 8. *Hu*: An ecstatic Sufi outcry. It refers to the divine breath.

You Are As You Are, line 3. Bayezid Bistami was a ninth-century Sufi saint who blended the Indian meditative way with the ecstatic Islamic *fana,* the state of being so dissolved in God that what is said is said by the divine presence. He wrote nothing, but many of his sayings are preserved. "How great is my glory!" "I came forth from Bayezid-ness as a snake from its skin. Then I looked and saw that lover and beloved are one."

Inside the Rose, line 2. *Sutur and Koshek*: Nevit Ergin tells me that these are still common names for animals in Turkey. No doubt the camel and calf moving by initiated the creation of the poem.

A World Dense with Greeting, line 38. I have taken the liberty of including greetings from around the world. *Teshekkür ederim*: Turkish for "thank you." Inquiring about the depth of one's well is a morning greeting of the Cherokees.

What Have You Been Drinking?, line 17. *Kaymaz, Sencer:* ordinary first names, probably actual people in the community.

Saladin. Saladin Zarkub the goldsmith in Konya who became Rumi's friend after Shams's disappearance. Rumi's son, Sultan Velad, married Saladin's daughter.

A NOTE ON THE TRANSLATION

Nevit Ergin has completed the massive project of bringing Rumi's *Divan* into English from Golpinarli's Turkish translation. Rumi is known and loved in Turkey through the work of Golpinarli. Dr. Ergin knew Professor Golpinarli and is a native Turkish speaker. He does not work from the original Persian; nor do I, of course. He plans to publish the entire twenty-one "meters" of the *Divan*. A *meter* is a non-chronological gathering of poems written in the same rhyme and rhythm. Ergin's English, then, is twice removed: from Rumi's Persian to Golpinarli's Turkish to English. I have worked from Dr. Ergin's translations to produce these very free, *thirdhand* versions. I hope the attunement to Rumi has not been lost in the relaying process. I feel the connection is a live one when I sit with Dr. Ergin, and I am honored that he has encouraged me to continue these re-workings from his texts. Nevit Ergin has moved back to Istanbul now. His texts are available from the organization he founded, The Society for Understanding Mevlana, 524 Cook St., Cordell, Okla. 73632 (877-218-6119).

Obviously, these (*The Glance*) poems are not literal or "faithful" translations, in the scholarly sense. There has been a lot of condensation and sometimes elaboration. But it is my hope these poems in English are true to the fire and ecstasy of the *ghazal*s in the *Divan*.

Nevit Ergin has been absorbed for over forty years in this work. He says, "Reading the *Divan* is like walking in a mine field: it blows your head, your heart, your soul." He quotes Rumi to explain: "Through annihilation of action, soul will be discovered. Through annihilation of attributes, absolute love will be experienced. At the end is annihilation of essence, which is annihilation within annihilation." The process involves a lot of remembering, a lot of contrition and austerity, Ergin says. "The joys of fellowship will come later." I deeply respect the service that Nevit Ergin has done. There is a sense of being inside a presence, or an absence, in his dedication to this work.

REFERENCES

The poems of this text are referenced below according to the meter and *ghazal* numbers in Nevit Ergin's texts, which refer to Golpinarli's Turkish translations, which are numbered according to Professor Bedi-uzzaman Furuzanfar's 1965 eight-volume edition of *Kulliyat-i Shams ya Divan-i Kabir*. "Meter," as it's being used here, refers to a collection of poems composed, in the Persian, in the same rhythm and the same rhyme scheme. In the notes below, *Mag.* refers to Nevit Ergin's *Magnificent One* (Burdett, N.Y.: Larson Publications, 1993). The following abbreviations refer to Ergin's Turkish sources: *HMM* = *Hezec Museddese Mahfuz*; *HM* = *Hezec-i Mekful*; *HS* = *Hezec Salim*; *GD* = Golpinarli's *Gul Deste*.

Jars of Springwater: meter 4, skipped *ghazal* number, verse 2390
The Taste of Morning: meter 2, *ghazal* 138
An Invisible Bee: 2, 93
A General Introductory Lecture: 4, 45
Hamza's Nothing: 2, 79
The Verge of Tears: 2, 107
Grainy Taste: 3, 27
Tambourine Feet: 3, 152
The Mirror Between Us: 3, 100
In Love that Long: 3, 176
Green from Inside: 4, 99